M000198880

Over the course of time, there have been so many changes in our days and in everything around us. But one thing always stays the same:

My feeling that you are
more than just a son...
you're an incredibly special one.

⑨ Lorrie Westfall

Blue Mountain Arts®

"The Language of the Heart…" series

For an Amazing Son

Marriage Is a Promise to Love

Mothers & Daughters

A Sister Is Forever

To a Beautiful Daughter

True Friendship Is a Gift

The Language of the Heart...

For an
Amazing
Son

A Blue Mountain Arts® Collection

Edited by Becky McKay

Blue Mountain Press™
Boulder, Colorado

Copyright © 2019 by Blue Mountain Arts, Inc.

All rights reserved. No part of this publication may be reproduced, stored in a retrieval system or transmitted in any form or by any means, electronic, mechanical, photocopying, recording or otherwise, without the written permission of the publisher.

We wish to thank Susan Polis Schutz for permission to reprint the following poems that appear in this publication: "To see you happy…," "A mother tries to provide her son…," "…a kite flying through the trees…," "We must make the world…," "My son…," and "I feel so fortunate to have you for a son…." Copyright © 1985, 1988, 2001, 2007 by Stephen Schutz and Susan Polis Schutz. All rights reserved.

Library of Congress Control Number: 2019936825
ISBN: 978-1-68088-294-0

▉ and Blue Mountain Press are registered in U.S. Patent and Trademark Office. Certain trademarks are used under license.

Acknowledgments appear on the last page.

Handmade paper used on cover made in Thailand.
Printed and assembled in China.
First Printing: 2019

✺ Interior of this book is printed on recycled paper.

Blue Mountain Arts, Inc.
P.O. Box 4549, Boulder, Colorado 80306

Contents

(Authors listed in order of first appearance)

Son, There Are So Many Things I Want to Tell You

You are strong and capable of taking on the world. You are brave and real and valued. Always appreciate the people around you, because you don't know how long they will be there. Trust in yourself no matter how hard the road ahead seems.

Wish on stars and believe in the magic of life. Go after your dreams and chase them down until they become realities in your days. Let your heart lead the way, and never be too proud to ask for a little help.

Most of all, know how much you are loved.

 Ashley Rice

How Did I Get So Lucky to Have You for a Son?

I have never doubted your choices, for they have always come from an intelligent, caring, and loving person.

You have shown me the extraordinary in the ordinary. You have taken flight to your dreams and proceeded full speed ahead. You're a winner in all areas of your life because you make the commitment to excellence.

Your winning attitude has led you to opportunities that have enriched your life. Making others feel comfortable is something that comes naturally to you. You are such a kind and gentle soul, always open to new opportunities.

Nothing makes a parent's heart fill with joy more than seeing their son succeed beyond expectations and living to his full potential.

 Kathryn Leibovich

If someone were to ask me
what has been my biggest
    accomplishment in life,
I would lift my head high
and speak from my heart
    with a parent's pride
as I said the words "my son."

⊙ Andrea Adaire Fischer

Being your parent has given me
happiness to the greatest degree
and warmth that fills my heart.
I am in awe that you came into my life
and made my dreams come true.

⊙ Barbara Cage

Son, You Are Amazing

You are your own person, and it's my privilege
to witness who you've grown up to be. You
may have started small and helpless in my
arms, but now I know you are capable of so
much. It has inspired me to watch you grow
brilliantly into yourself. I have always had such
high hopes for you, and you continue to exceed
them with the incredible person you are.

Amy L. Kuo

You're not just a fantastic son. You're a tremendous,
rare, and extraordinary person. All the different
facets of your life — the ones you reveal to the rest
of the world and the ones known only to those
you're close to — are so impressive. And as people
look even deeper, I know they can't help but see
how wonderful you are inside.

Douglas Pagels

To see you happy —
laughing and joking
smiling and content
striving toward goals of your own
accomplishing what you set out to do
having fun
capable of loving and being loved
is what I always wished for you
Today I thought about your
        handsome face
and felt your excitement for life
and your genuine happiness
and I burst with pride
as I realized that my dreams
        for you have come true
What an extraordinary person
        you have become
and as you continue to grow
please remember always
how very much
I love you

Susan Polis Schutz

When I Look at You...

When I look at you…
I see an exceptional person
with so many wonderful qualities —
someone who is smart, determined,
capable, reliable, persistent,
and so much more.

When I look at you…
I see someone who is destined
to accomplish great things in life —
and I see someone who deserves
all the amazing things
that will be coming your way.

When I look at you…
it fills my heart with smiles and joy
to see what you've accomplished —
and the special person you've become.

 Jason Blume

When I look at you, I see years of memories and decades of potential. You have already changed my world in spectacular ways, and now I see you impact the rest of the world in wonderful ways as well.

But though I see the best parts of you, please know I never expect you to be perfect... no one is. I am just so glad that you are perfectly you. A parent couldn't ask for more.

Amy L. Kuo

Advice for My Son

Savor life. Not just the usual pleasures, but everything and everyone. The stranger you meet on the bus. The sunshine that hits your face as you walk. The quiet of the morning. Time with a loved one. Time alone....

Don't be afraid to make mistakes. They are some of the best teachers. Instead, learn to be okay with mistakes, learn to learn from them, and learn to shrug them off so they don't affect your profound confidence in who you are.

You need no one else to make you happy or validate you. You don't need a boss to tell you that you're great at what you do. You don't need a boyfriend/girlfriend to tell you that you're lovable. You don't need your friends' approval. Having loved ones and friends in your life is amazing, but know who you are first.

Learn to be good at change. Change is the one constant in life. You will suffer by trying to hold on to things. Learn to let go (meditation helps with this skill), and learn to have a flexible mind. Don't get stuck in what you're comfortable with; don't shut out what's new and uncomfortable.

Open your heart. Life is amazing if you don't shut it out. Other people are amazing. Open your heart, be willing to take the wounds that come with an open heart, and you will experience the best of life.

Let love be your rule. Success, selfishness, righteousness… these are not good rules to live by. Love family, friends, coworkers, strangers, your brothers and sisters in humanity. Love even those who think they're your enemy. Love the animals we treat as food and objects. Most of all, love yourself.

And always know, no matter what: I love you with every particle of my being.

@ Leo Babauta

Never Give Up

When life looks like a mountain that is impossible to climb, just remember how incredible you are.

You have all the resources you need to see you through. You have optimism and a graceful way of dealing with adversity.

You are a courageous person who has faced challenges before and always come bouncing back with a smile on your face. You are resilient and courageous, especially when you feel doubtful and uncertain. It is in these times that you show your true strength of character.

When life tests you, remember that you are so much bigger than you think you are. Your buoyant spirit will win once again. Whatever it takes, you can do it.

 Lynda Field

Even when you get a little discouraged, don't allow yourself to give up.

If you back away from obstacles that appear before you because they seem too difficult, then you're not being true to yourself. Don't be afraid to take risks, or even to fail. It isn't about winning or losing. It's about loving yourself enough and believing in who you are that counts in the end.

⑨ T. L. Nash

Life is what you make of it, and the challenges that come your way are opportunities to right what is wrong. Don't get discouraged, and don't give up. You have it all inside yourself, and you can overcome anything if you put your mind to it.

⑨ Paula Michele Adams

Go Out into the World and Make It Your Own

Within the soul of every man
lives the little boy he once was —
a boy who looked at the world with
eyes full of wonder, who always
believed in "once upon a time,"
and who planned to conquer
the world someday.

ℰ Edmund O'Neill

Twenty years from now you will be more disappointed
by the things you didn't do than by the ones you did
do. So throw off the bowlines. Sail away from the safe
harbor. Catch the trade winds in your sails. Explore.
Dream. Discover.

ℰ Mark Twain

There are so many new horizons ahead. In the blink of an eye, sons are out the door and off to college, off to jobs, and eventually on to setting up their own homes and tending to their families and future lives. It's a time when parents hope and pray that all the values and lessons they tried to instill will help to light the way for the journey ahead.

And I am no exception: I want great things for you, too... and I have an enormous amount of faith in your ability to make your life a happy one. You take with you, everywhere you go, a supply of confidence, common sense, ability, determination, understanding, wisdom, and so many attributes that just sparkle inside you. You know how to make the right choices, and I know that you will.

@ Douglas Pagels

Remember...
You Can Always
Come Back Home

From family, we draw love,
   friendship, moral support,
and the fulfillment of every
   special need within our hearts.
In a family, we are connected to
   an ever-present source
of sunny moments, smiles and laughter,
understanding and encouragement,
and hugs that help us grow
   in confidence all along life's path.

Wherever we are, whatever we're doing,
whenever we really need to feel especially
   loved, befriended, supported,
and cared for in the greatest way,
our hearts can turn to family
and find the very best
   always waiting for us.

Ⓖ Barbara J. Hall

When life gets hard, come home. When you find yourself in a sticky situation, come home. When it's just all too much, come home. Friends will come and go, but family is forever. (Invest wisely.) Always have your brother's back in public, even if he's wrong... we'll sort things out when you get home. Remember, Mom and Dad are here for you, and this place we call home is a safe place. In all seriousness, there is no food like a mama's comfort food. It's science. When in doubt, just come home.

Christen Siegmund Spratt

Home is the place where,
when you have to go there,
they have to take you in.

Robert Frost

A Mother and Her Son

A mother tries to provide her son
with insight into the important things in life
in order to make his life
as happy and fulfilling as possible

A mother tries to teach her son
to be kind and generous toward other people
to be honest and forthright at all times
to be fair, treating men and women equally
to respect and learn from older people
to know himself very well
to understand his strong and weak points
to accept criticism and learn from his mistakes
to have many interests to pursue
to have many goals to follow
to work hard to reach these goals

A mother tries to teach her son
to have a strong set of beliefs
to listen to his intelligence
to laugh and enjoy life
to appreciate the beauty of nature
to express his feelings openly
    and honestly at all times
to realize that love is the best emotion
    that anyone can have
to value the family unit
    as the basis of all stability

If I have provided you with an insight
into most of these things
then I have succeeded as a mother
in what I hoped to accomplish in raising you
If many of these things slipped by
while we were all so busy
I have a feeling that you know them anyway
And as a proud mother and as a friend
I will always continue to love and support
everything you are and everything you do
I am always here for you, Son

❧ Susan Polis Schutz

You won't remember the way I stood in the bathroom late that night in labor with you, fearfully and excitedly gazing up at the moon, knowing I was going to bring you into the world soon, and whispering to you, "We can do this."

You won't remember the way you looked at me right after you were born or the way I pulled you up next to my heart and marveled "Hi, baby" in your ear.

You won't remember the way you healed my broken spirit. The way you completed my heart. I was weak before I had you, and you made me whole again.

You won't remember the way I proudly watched you everywhere we went. You were always the most beautiful boy in the room to me.

You won't remember the way you made me laugh with all of the silly things you did. I saw how kind your heart was.

You won't remember the way I would brush the hair off of your forehead and the way you'd look up at me. Without any words, our souls could touch and say everything to each other that words couldn't.

You won't remember the tickle fests we had and how I always cheated so I could hold you close and cover your salty little face in kisses.

You won't remember all the times I went to bed at night and felt such fear being your mother: Am I doing okay? Have I messed up too many times already? Can I be the kind of mother he needs?

You won't remember the way my heart broke and grew a little bigger each time you passed a milestone, watching the sand fall through the hourglass while feeling overjoyed witnessing you expand and grow.

You won't remember the way I would hold your little feet in my hands, imagining how much bigger than my own feet they will one day grow, and how I will have to let you go.

You won't remember, but I will… and I'll hold these memories in my heart for the both of us.

 Jessica Dimas

A Father and His Son

Fathers are different from mothers. They look different, they sound different, they play in a different way, and they usually have a different approach to raising children than a mother does. And that's a good thing. A boy learns from his father, without even realizing he's doing it, what a man is and does. He learns about masculinity, about what men like and don't like. Many adult men report that they either wanted to be "just like my dad" — or wanted to be his exact opposite. Fathers undoubtedly have a powerful influence on their growing sons, and it begins from the moment of birth.

ⓒ Cheryl L. Erwin

If you ever become a father, I think the strangest and strongest sensation of your life will be hearing for the first time the thin cry of your own child. For a moment you have the strange feeling of being double; but there is something more... perhaps the echo in a man's heart of all the sensations felt by all the fathers and mothers... at a similar instant in the past....

No man can possibly know what life means, what the world means, what anything means, until he has a child and loves it. Then the whole universe changes and nothing will ever again seem exactly as it seemed before.

 Lafcadio Hearn

I was the first to hold you. This is not to say that the doctor didn't handle you and the nurse didn't swaddle you, but I was the first to really hold you. To snuggle you and look in your face and realize that we had the same nose, same hands, same browline, and I wondered if we'd share the same frustrations. I wondered if we'd have similar personalities and frustrations and passions, and in that moment, when I saw how much of me was in you, I felt warm.

I felt confident and I didn't know why, but over the years I have begun to understand that it was the innate understanding between a father and a son.

It's the knowledge that even though you will grow up at a different time and in a different place, we still share similar blood, and with my understanding of myself, I have a good head start on understanding you.

The funny thing is, though, even with all that... I'm still scared that I'm doing it wrong. I'm always afraid that I'm going to make the wrong decision, push you too hard, or say some stupid thing that pushes you away....

I want you to love me as much as I love you, and I'm not sure what that looks like. Perhaps you never will. I don't know. I've never experienced it. But what I do know is that every day with you I get back a little bit of what I lost with my own father. Every time we play basketball in the yard, do work in the garden, go swimming, read stories, or hang out on the sofa and watch silly movies from the '80s, I get with you what I always wanted from my father. And when I read what I just wrote, it sounds selfish. But at the same time, it's ironic. I was so scared of having a child because I never had a father. I was afraid I'd be lost. But what ended up happening was me regaining something I'd always longed for: a father-son relationship....

Whether you are eight or eighteen or twenty-eight, I will always love you. You will always be my son. You are a bigger gift to me than I think you will ever know.

⟲ Clint Edwards

A Son Is...

...a baby who is wished wondrous love; a child who is wished endless joy; a boy who is wished understanding and ever-widening circles of knowledge and friendship.

...a teenager who is wished strength in any surroundings, courage in every circumstance, and a recognition of the wonders that await his tomorrows.

...a man, with paths to walk, with bridges to cross, with mountains to climb. A son is an amazing combination of all of these things, and he's quietly thanked, every day of his life, for the priceless joy he brings.

 Douglas Pagels

...the shining light of his parents' hopes and dreams. He is a young man who makes life's moments so beautiful with the miracle of all he has been, and the treasure of everything he will become.

Terry Bairnson

...a kite flying through the trees
a tadpole turning into a frog
a dandelion in the wind
a mischievous smile
laughing eyes
a scrape on the knees
a wonder
an excitement, a burst of energy
an animation
a spirited breeze
A son is love
and everything beautiful

— Susan Polis Schutz

...your past and your future. He is hopes and
dreams that have made it through each and every
disappointment and failure. In your heart, your
son is precious and treasured.

— Barbara Cage

...a gift no one could ever
put a price on and
the reason why
my life is so wonderful.

— Renate M. Braddy

As a child, you were every bit boy —
a seeker and explorer,
with dirty elbows and knees,
and countless adventures under your belt.

You wore a smile that warmed my heart,
and your mischievous ways
always kept me on my toes.
How I laughed at the things I'd find
in your pockets when I did laundry!

You were an innovator,
always looking to fix, create,
and find solutions to things.
You were curious by nature,
and your spirit was unstoppable!

Well, some things haven't changed.
Your smile still warms my heart, and
your inquisitive and creative nature
has brought you boundless
achievements and success in life.

I hope you know how proud you've made me.
When I look at you, I see someone
who is strong, confident, and capable,
yet humble, compassionate, and kind.

I will always cherish you, Son.
Being your parent has been
the greatest joy,
the greatest blessing,
and the greatest adventure of my life.

 Kerrianne McGrath

If —

If you can keep your head when all about you
    Are losing theirs and blaming it on you,
If you can trust yourself when all men doubt you,
    But make allowance for their doubting too;
If you can wait and not be tired by waiting,
    Or being lied about, don't deal in lies,
Or being hated, don't give way to hating,
    And yet don't look too good, nor talk too wise:

If you can dream — and not make dreams your master;
    If you can think — and not make thoughts your aim,
If you can meet with Triumph and Disaster
    And treat those two impostors just the same;
If you can bear to hear the truth you've spoken
    Twisted by knaves to make a trap for fools,
Or watch the things you gave your life to, broken,
    And stoop and build 'em up with worn-out tools:

If you can make one heap of all your winnings
     And risk it on one turn of pitch-and-toss,
And lose, and start again at your beginnings
     And never breathe a word about your loss;
If you can force your heart and nerve and sinew
     To serve your turn long after they are gone,
And so hold on when there is nothing in you
     Except the Will which says to them: "Hold on!"

If you can talk with crowds and keep your virtue,
     Or walk with Kings — nor lose the common touch,
If neither foes nor loving friends can hurt you,
     If all men count with you, but none too much;
If you can fill the unforgiving minute
     With sixty seconds' worth of distance run,
Yours is the Earth and everything that's in it,
     And — which is more — you'll be a Man, my son!

Rudyard Kipling

What Does It Mean to Be a Man?

A man is as great as the dreams he dreams,
　　As great as the love he bears;
As great as the values he redeems,
　　And the happiness he shares.
A man is as great as the thoughts he thinks,
　　As the worth he has attained;
As the fountains at which his spirit drinks,
　　And the insight he has gained.
A man is as great as the truth he speaks,
　　As great as the help he gives,
As great as the destiny he seeks,
　　As great as the life he lives.

C. E. Flynn

The strongest man today is the most vulnerable. If you're able to be self-aware of what you feel and what you want and you don't have to fake anything or try to keep up the image that society puts on you... if you are who you are and you're able to embrace that, you're a man.

Alex Rodriguez,
TEDx speaker

As a man, you will face challenging times; it happens to all of us. What defines you is how you respond to that adversity. It's normal to be scared — just don't stop moving forward.

Charles J. Orlando

A Prayer
for My Son

I pray that your faith will always stay strong and bravely take you through every crisis, that hope will always blaze inside you — even when life seems bleakest — and that peace will fill your mind, heart, and spirit with every breath you take.

I pray that love will hold you close with each new day and remind you that you are never alone. I pray that joy will always come your way, so that you will experience life with all the delight of the little boy who still lives inside you. I pray that your kindnesses will shine in the smiles of the people whose lives you've touched.

I pray that your confidence will always be reborn whenever you take a nasty fall — and that you'll stand tall when others don't believe in your dreams, passions, and beliefs.

I pray that healing will come to you completely when you are injured — physically or emotionally — and that family and friends who love and support you will help you recover much sooner.

I pray that forgiveness will heal your heart when others cause you distress, that you'll know you are worthy of happiness and success, and that you'll be blessed with a sunny mind, heart, and attitude. I pray you will always keep close to your goals and stay focused on reaching for the stars you choose. And I pray you know I will always love you with every prayer, with all the love I have gained in raising you from a wonderful boy to a very special man.

 Jacqueline Schiff

Be True to
Who You Are

What are the values, in this moment, to instill in a son? It's a lot to think about. But in the end... I think the answer is pretty simple. I think you tell him...: *Be yourself. Be good, and try to be great — but always be yourself.*

Stephen Curry

Be true to yourself in the paths that you choose. Follow your talents and passions; don't take the roads others say you must follow because they are the most popular. Take the paths where your talents will thrive — the ones that will keep your spirits alive with enthusiasm and everlasting joy.

Jacqueline Schiff

Honor who you are, what you have, and where you're going. Open the door to the unexpected. Welcome every day and make room for the joy that's coming your way. Let happiness be your compass and the universe be your guide. Write your own story and cherish who you are. Be your own inspiration. Remember that it's not how far you still have to go, but how far you've already come.

Linda E. Knight

Respect Others...
Respect Yourself

Respect comes from the understanding that others are separate from us. They are their own beings, entitled to freedom of thought, word, opinion, action, and values. They are not ours to change or boss around.

People can only thrive when given enough space to express themselves in the way that they want. When you treat them with respect, you're saying, "You're important, you're smart, and you're strong enough to find your own way."

@ Latesha Randall

As human beings, our job in life is to help people realize how rare and valuable each one of us really is, that each of us has something that no one else has — or ever will have — something inside that is unique to all time. It's our job to encourage each other to discover that uniqueness and to provide ways of developing its expression.

Fred Rogers

We must make the world
a place where
love dominates our hearts
nature sets the standard for beauty
simplicity and honesty are
the essence of our relationships
kindness guides our actions
and everyone respects one another

Susan Polis Schutz

Stay Strong

Strength isn't always measured by
    success and happiness.
Strong people aren't born that way,
and strength isn't inherited.
It is most often gained through
    suffering;
you are made stronger by the people
and circumstances that try your patience,
the questions you can't answer,
and the times you are forced to rely
    on others.
Strength is gradually acquired through
    the years;
it is built like a foundation —
everything is pieced together
    bit by bit,
until one day you know who you are
and what you're made of.

                                 Cindee Fuller

My son
you are strong enough
to counter any problems that occur —
naysayers who tell you that you can't
disappointments that leave you frustrated
stinging words of others that hurt
    your feelings
obstacles in your path that make you
    want to quit
relationships that are sad or unhealthy

And you are strong enough
to enjoy the beautiful aspects of life —
people who encourage you
friends who really care about you
kind and complimentary words of others
highlights on your individual path
    that are exciting
relationships that are worthwhile and deep
literature, music and art
solitude and nature
and your own
independence and happiness

 Susan Polis Schutz

You are not bound by the opinions
    of others
but rather what you hold to be true
    in your heart

Some will remember past mistakes
but the ones who treasure you as a
    human being
will understand that we all have failed
    at some point

Life constantly pulls you
encouraging you to be a little braver
pushing you to become stronger
while gently whispering to
    "follow your heart"

It is easy to give opinions
but you are who you are
Nowhere does it say
that two hearts beat exactly the same

It is generally the ones who have
    lost the most
loved the most
and forgiven the most
that are misunderstood

You are not who you are by opinion
You are who you are because you
    have chosen
to believe in yourself

Lisa Mae Huddleston

I Love You, Son

I feel so fortunate to have you for a son
I love your bright face
when we talk seriously about the world
I love your smile
when you laugh at the inconsistencies in the world
I love your eyes
when you are showing emotion
I love your mind
when you are discovering new ideas
and creating dreams to follow
Many people tell me that
they cannot talk to their children
that they cannot wait for them to leave home
I want you to know
that I enjoy you so much and
I look forward to any time we can spend together
Not only are you my adored son
but you are also my friend
I am so proud of you
my son and
I love you

© Susan Polis Schutz

All throughout my life, I have realized over and over: I've never been more blessed than when I was given the gift of being your parent.

All throughout your life, you have amazed me and impressed me and given me thousands of reasons to love you more than I already do.

Over the course of time, there have been so many changes in our days and in everything around us. But one thing always stays the same:

My feeling that you are
more than just a son...
you're an incredibly special one.

 Lorrie Westfall

You'll Always Be
My Little Boy

Today I wish I could go back. I wish I could go back and hold you as an infant. I wish I could smell your skin and rock you just a little longer. I wish I could be still and feel that moment just one more time.

When I look at pictures of you in your toddler years with your round cheeks and pudgy hands, I smile. Inside my heart breaks a little bit because I wish I could squeeze you as you ask me a billion questions in your tiny voice, just one more time.

You're lying on the couch next to me with your giant feet protruding under a fleece blanket and a book in your hands. *How and where has this time gone*, I think. I can remember when you were just a whisper and a glimmer of a dream. And here you are, this giant boy that will be a man when I blink just a few more times.

You've become gifted in the art of rolling your eyes when you disagree and saying, "Mom, just listen to me for a second...." I'm not always good at listening; I know that. We don't always agree, and sometimes I don't handle our disagreements very well; I'm working on that.

But no matter what, you're still my little boy.... You'll be my little boy forever.

Jessica Johnston

If I Could Have One Wish in All the World...

I'd wish that you would
always be happy, forever healthy,
and that your life would be filled
with all the things that bring you
laughter and love.

I'd wish for you a life where
your dreams come true
and your goals are achieved,
where there are no tears
that I can't wipe from your face
and make everything okay again.

I hope you will always know
that I am thinking about you
and forever wanting nothing more
than your complete happiness
in life.

It's your happiness that brings
me such immense joy,
because you are my son
and I love you so much.

 Shelly Gross

The Bond Between Parent and Son Lasts a Lifetime

The bond between parent and son
is a special one.
It remains unchanged
by time or distance.
It is the purest love —
unconditional and true.
It is understanding of any situation
and forgiving of any mistake.

The bond between parent and son
creates a support that is constant
while everything else changes.
It is a friendship based on mutual
love, respect,
and a genuine liking of each other
as a person.

It is knowing that no matter where
    you go or who you are,
there is someone who truly loves you
and is always there to support and
    console you.
When a situation seems impossible,
you make it through together
by holding on to each other.

The bond between parent and son
is strong enough to withstand harsh words
    and hurt feelings,
for it is smart enough to always
see the love beyond the words.
It is brave enough to always speak the truth,
even when lies would be easier.
It is always there — anytime, anywhere —
whenever it is needed.
It is a gift held in the heart and in the soul,
and it cannot be taken away
or exchanged for another.
To possess this love is a treasure
that makes life more valuable.

 Stephanie Douglass

Acknowledgments

We gratefully acknowledge the permission granted by the following authors, publishers, and authors' representatives to reprint poems or excerpts in this publication: Jason Blume for "When I look at you...." Copyright © 2016 by Jason Blume. All rights reserved. Christen Siegmund Spratt for "When life gets hard..." from "Raising My Teen to Leave Me: 13 Pieces of Advice for Him on His 13th Birthday," *Christen Spratt* (blog), August 27, 2017, http://christenspratt.com/13-pieces-of-advice-for-my-son-on-his-13th-birthday. Copyright © 2017 by Christen Siegmund Spratt. All rights reserved. Jessica Dimas for "You won't remember..." from "You Won't Remember, But I Will," *Pig and Dac* (blog), September 8, 2014, http://piganddac.com/you-wont-remember-but-i-will/. Copyright © 2014 by Jessica Dimas. All rights reserved. Adams Media, an imprint of Simon & Schuster, Inc., for "Fathers are different..." from THE EVERYTHING PARENT'S GUIDE TO RAISING BOYS, 2nd edition, by Cheryl L. Erwin. Copyright © 2006, 2011 by Simon & Schuster, Inc. All rights reserved. Clint Edwards for "I was the first..." from "To My Son on His 8th Birthday," *byclintedwards* (blog), March 20, 2015, http://www.byclintedwards.com/2015/03/to-my-son-on-his-8th-birthday.html/. Copyright © 2015 by Clint Edwards. All rights reserved. Kerrianne McGrath for "As a child, you were...." Copyright © 2019 by Kerrianne McGrath. All rights reserved. *Unconventional Life* for "The strongest man today..." by Alex Rodriguez from "Ep:104 The 'Evolved' Man: Embracing Authenticity as a Man," *Unconventional Life Show* (podcast), October 2017, produced by Jules Schroeder, http://www.unconventionallifeshow.com/ep104-the-evolved-man-embracing-authenticity-as-a-man/. Copyright © 2017 by Alex Rodriguez. All rights reserved. Charles J. Orlando for "As a man, you will..." from "11 Lessons for My Graduating Son," originally posted on *Your Tango* (blog), June 14, 2014. Copyright © 2014 by Charles J. Orlando. All rights reserved. Stephen Curry and The Players' Tribune, Inc. for "What are the values..." from "This Is Personal," *The Players' Tribune*, August 26, 2018, https://www.theplayerstribune.com/en-us/articles/stephen-curry-womens-equality. Copyright © 2018 by Stephen Curry. All rights reserved. Linda E. Knight for "Honor who you are...." Copyright © 2019 by Linda E. Knight. All rights reserved. Latesha Randall for "Respect comes from the understanding..." from THE TO-BE LIST. Copyright © 2017 by Latesha Randall. All rights reserved. Viking Books, an imprint of Penguin Publishing Group, a division of Penguin Random House LLC, for "As human beings..." from YOU ARE SPECIAL: WORDS OF WISDOM FROM AMERICA'S MOST BELOVED NEIGHBOR by Fred Rogers. Copyright © 1994 Family Communications, Inc. All rights reserved. Cindee Fuller for "Strength isn't always measured by...." Copyright © 2019 by Cindee Fuller. All rights reserved. Lisa Mae Huddleston for "You are not bound by...." Copyright © 2019 by Lisa Mae Huddleston. All rights reserved. Jessica Johnston for "Today I wish I could go back..." from "Dear Son, You'll Always Be My Little Boy," *Wonderoak* (blog), July 29, 2018, https://wonderoak.com/2018/07/29/dear-son-youll-always-be-my-little-boy/. Copyright © 2018 by Jessica Johnston. All rights reserved.

A careful effort has been made to trace the ownership of selections used in this anthology in order to obtain permission to reprint copyrighted material and give proper credit to the copyright owners. If any error or omission has occurred, it is completely inadvertent, and we would like to make corrections in future editions provided that written notification is made to the publisher:

BLUE MOUNTAIN ARTS, INC., P.O. Box 4549, Boulder, Colorado 80306